COMPOSER
SHOWCASE
HAL LEONARD
STUDENT PIANO LIBRARY

Christmas Jazz

SIX CAROLS FOR PIANO SOLO

ARRANGED BY MIKE SPRINGER

CONTENTS

Edited by J. Mark Baker

ISBN 978-0-634-08465-2

HAL•LEONARD®
CORPORATION
7777 W. BLUEMOUND RD. P.O. BOX 13819 MILWAUKEE, WI 53213

In Australia Contact:
Hal Leonard Australia Pty. Ltd.
22 Taunton Drive P.O. Box 5130
Cheltenham East, 3192 Victoria, Australia
Email: ausadmin@halleonard.com

Visit Hal Leonard Online at
www.halleonard.com

Away In A Manger

Music by James R. Murray
Arranged by Mike Springer

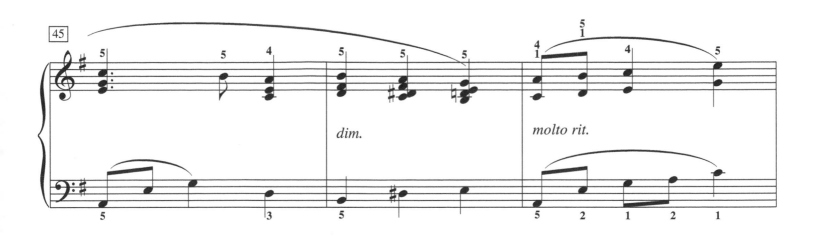

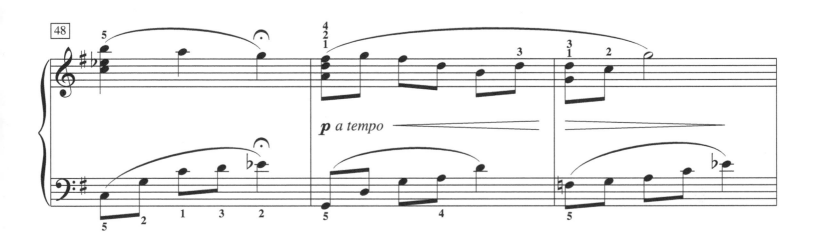

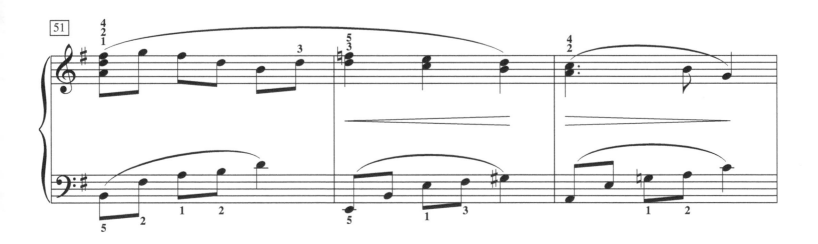

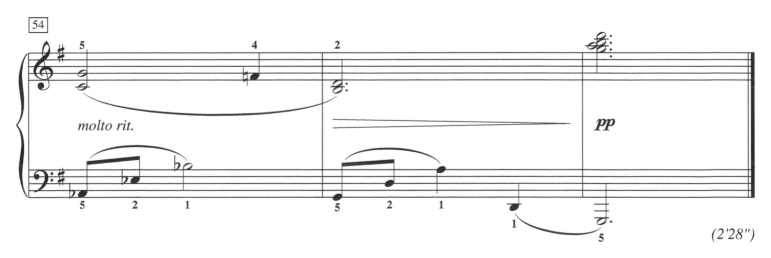

(2'28")

Deck The Hall

Traditional Welsh Carol
Arranged by Mike Springer

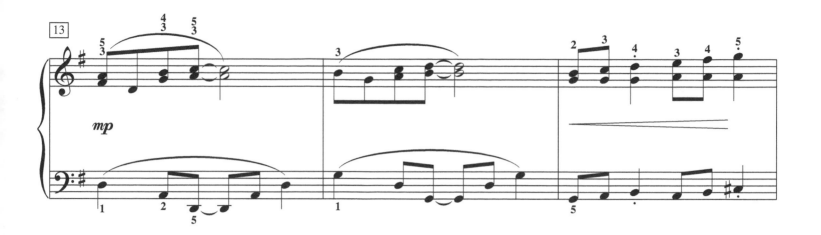

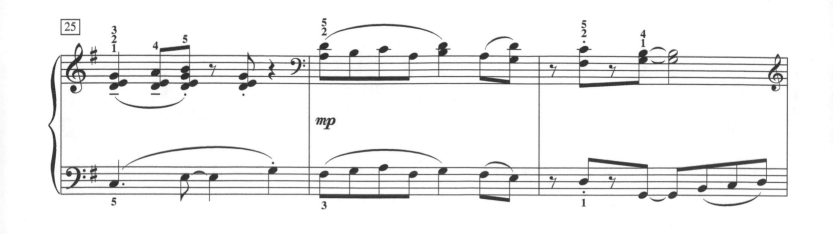

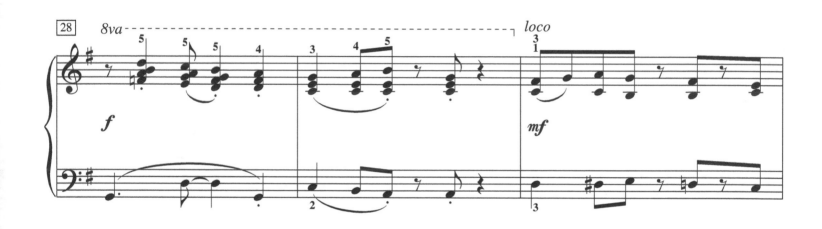

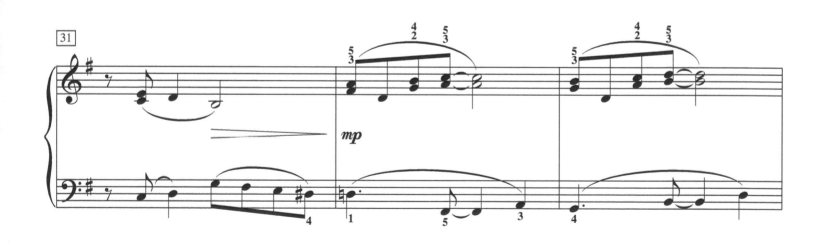

8

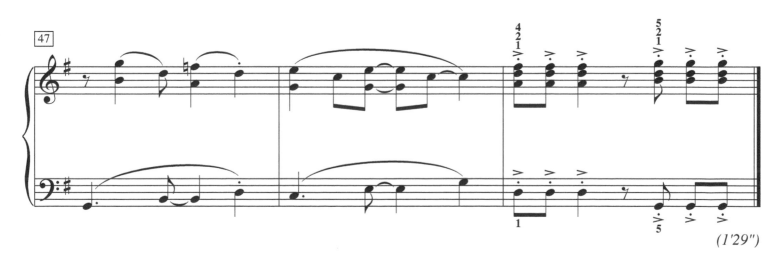

(1'29")

9

Jingle Bells

Music by James Pierpont
Arranged by Mike Springer

Quick Ragtime feel (♩ = 100) (♫ = ♩♪)

Silent Night

Music by Franz Gruber
Arranged by Mike Springer

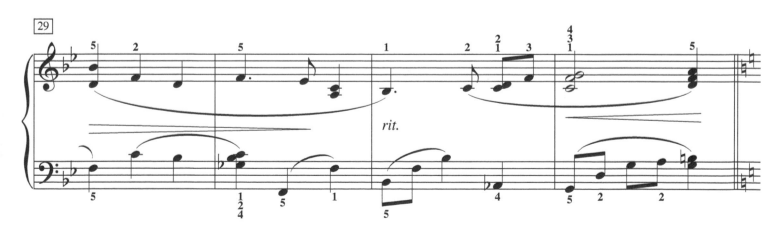

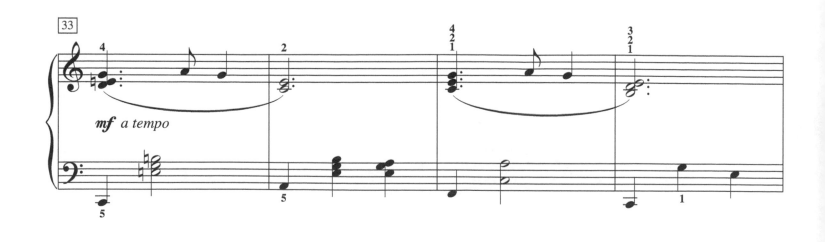

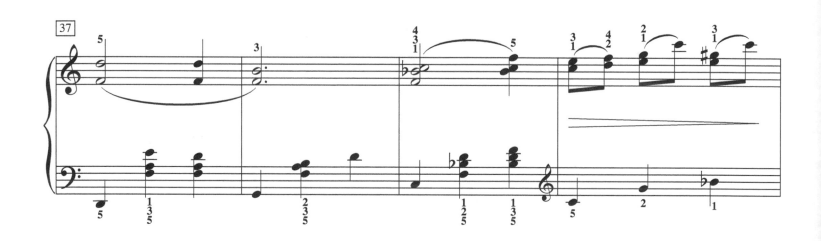

(3'16")

It Came Upon The Midnight Clear

Music by Richard Storrs Willis
Arranged by Mike Springer

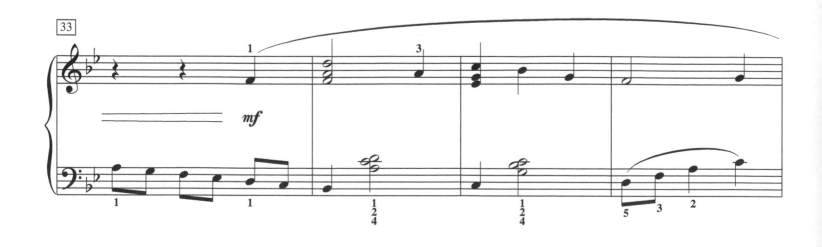

(1'56")

We Wish You A Merry Christmas

Traditional English Carol
Arranged by Mike Springer

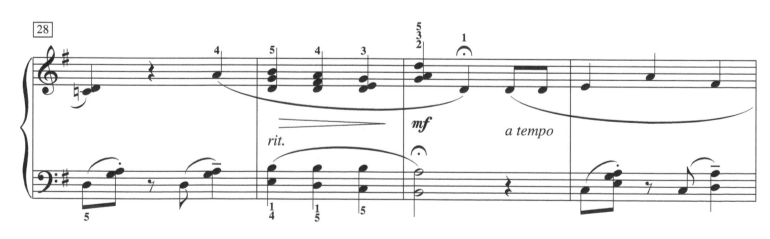

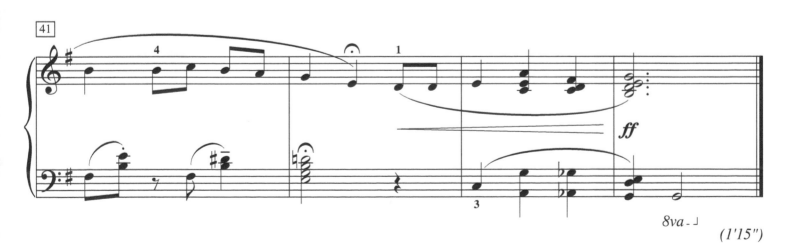

8va - ┘

(1'15")

This series showcases great original piano music from our **Hal Leonard Student Piano Library** family of composers. Carefully graded for easy selection.

BILL BOYD

JAZZ BITS (AND PIECES)
Early Intermediate Level
00290312 11 Solos.......................$7.99

JAZZ DELIGHTS
Intermediate Level
00240435 11 Solos.......................$8.99

JAZZ FEST
Intermediate Level
00240436 10 Solos.......................$8.99

JAZZ PRELIMS
Early Elementary Level
00290032 12 Solos.......................$7.99

JAZZ SKETCHES
Intermediate Level
00220001 8 Solos.......................$8.99

JAZZ STARTERS
Elementary Level
00290425 10 Solos.......................$8.99

JAZZ STARTERS II
Late Elementary Level
00290434 11 Solos.......................$7.99

JAZZ STARTERS III
Late Elementary Level
00290465 12 Solos.......................$8.99

THINK JAZZ!
Early Intermediate Level
00290417 Method Book............$12.99

TONY CARAMIA

JAZZ MOODS
Intermediate Level
00296728 8 Solos.......................$6.95

SUITE DREAMS
Intermediate Level
00296775 4 Solos.......................$6.99

SONDRA CLARK

DAKOTA DAYS
Intermediate Level
00296521 5 Solos.......................$6.95

FLORIDA FANTASY SUITE
Intermediate Level
00296766 3 Duets.......................$7.95

THREE ODD METERS
Intermediate Level
00296472 3 Duets.......................$6.95

MATTHEW EDWARDS

CONCERTO FOR YOUNG PIANISTS
FOR 2 PIANOS, FOUR HANDS
Intermediate Level Book/CD
00296356 3 Movements $19.99

CONCERTO NO. 2 IN G MAJOR
FOR 2 PIANOS, 4 HANDS
Intermediate Level Book/CD
00296670 3 Movements............$17.99

PHILLIP KEVEREN

MOUSE ON A MIRROR
Late Elementary Level
00296361 5 Solos.......................$8.99

MUSICAL MOODS
Elementary/Late Elementary Level
00296714 7 Solos.......................$6.99

SHIFTY-EYED BLUES
Late Elementary Level
00296374 5 Solos.......................$7.99

CAROL KLOSE

THE BEST OF CAROL KLOSE
Early to Late Intermediate Level
00146151 15 Solos.....................$12.99

CORAL REEF SUITE
Late Elementary Level
00296354 7 Solos.......................$7.50

DESERT SUITE
Intermediate Level
00296667 6 Solos.......................$7.99

FANCIFUL WALTZES
Early Intermediate Level
00296473 5 Solos.......................$7.95

GARDEN TREASURES
Late Intermediate Level
00296787 5 Solos.......................$8.50

ROMANTIC EXPRESSIONS
Intermediate to Late Intermediate Level
00296923 5 Solos.......................$8.99

WATERCOLOR MINIATURES
Early Intermediate Level
00296848 7 Solos.......................$7.99

JENNIFER LINN

AMERICAN IMPRESSIONS
Intermediate Level
00296471 6 Solos.......................$8.99

ANIMALS HAVE FEELINGS TOO
Early Elementary/Elementary Level
00147789 8 Solos.......................$8.99

AU CHOCOLAT
Late Elementary/Early Intermediate Level
00298110 7 Solos.......................$8.99

CHRISTMAS IMPRESSIONS
Intermediate Level
00296706 8 Solos.......................$8.99

JUST PINK
Elementary Level
00296722 9 Solos.......................$8.99

LES PETITES IMAGES
Late Elementary Level
00296664 7 Solos.......................$8.99

LES PETITES IMPRESSIONS
Intermediate Level
00296355 6 Solos.......................$8.99

REFLECTIONS
Late Intermediate Level
00296843 5 Solos.......................$8.99

TALES OF MYSTERY
Intermediate Level
00296769 6 Solos.......................$8.99

LYNDA LYBECK-ROBINSON

ALASKA SKETCHES
Early Intermediate Level
00119637 8 Solos.......................$8.99

AN AWESOME ADVENTURE
Late Elementary Level
00137563 8 Solos.......................$7.99

FOR THE BIRDS
Early Intermediate/Intermediate Level
00237078 9 Solos.......................$8.99

WHISPERING WOODS
Late Elementary Level
00275905 9 Solos.......................$8.99

MONA REJINO

CIRCUS SUITE
Late Elementary Level
00296665 5 Solos.......................$8.99

COLOR WHEEL
Early Intermediate Level
00201951 6 Solos.......................$9.99

IMPRESIONES DE ESPAÑA
Intermediate Level
00337520 6 Solos.......................$8.99

IMPRESSIONS OF NEW YORK
Intermediate Level
00364212...............................$8.99

JUST FOR KIDS
Elementary Level
00296840 8 Solos.......................$7.99

MERRY CHRISTMAS MEDLEYS
Intermediate Level
00296799 5 Solos.......................$8.99

MINIATURES IN STYLE
Intermediate Level
00148088 6 Solos.......................$8.99

PORTRAITS IN STYLE
Early Intermediate Level
00296507 6 Solos.......................$8.99

EUGÉNIE ROCHEROLLE

CELEBRATION SUITE
Intermediate Level
00152724 3 Duets.......................$8.99

ENCANTOS ESPAÑOLES (SPANISH DELIGHTS)
Intermediate Level
00125451 6 Solos.......................$8.99

JAMBALAYA
Intermediate Level
00296654 2 Pianos, 8 Hands.....$12.99
00296725 2 Pianos, 4 Hands.......$7.95

JEROME KERN CLASSICS
Intermediate Level
00296577 10 Solos...................$12.99

LITTLE BLUES CONCERTO
Early Intermediate Level
00142801 2 Pianos, 4 Hands......$12.99

TOUR FOR TWO
Late Elementary Level
00296832 6 Duets.......................$9.99

TREASURES
Late Elementary/Early Intermediate Level
00296924 7 Solos.......................$8.99

JEREMY SISKIND

BIG APPLE JAZZ
Intermediate Level
00278209 8 Solos.......................$8.99

MYTHS AND MONSTERS
Late Elementary/Early Intermediate Level
00148148 9 Solos.......................$8.99

CHRISTOS TSITSAROS

DANCES FROM AROUND THE WORLD
Early Intermediate Level
00296688 7 Solos.......................$8.99

FIVE SUMMER PIECES
Late Intermediate/Advanced Level
00361235 5 Solos.....................$12.99

LYRIC BALLADS
Intermediate/Late Intermediate Level
00102404 6 Solos.......................$8.99

POETIC MOMENTS
Intermediate Level
00296403 8 Solos.......................$8.99

SEA DIARY
Early Intermediate Level
00253486 9 Solos.......................$8.99

SONATINA HUMORESQUE
Late Intermediate Level
00296772 3 Movements............$6.99

SONGS WITHOUT WORDS
Intermediate Level
00296506 9 Solos.......................$9.99

THREE PRELUDES
Early Advanced Level
00130747 3 Solos.......................$8.99

THROUGHOUT THE YEAR
Late Elementary Level
00296723 12 Duets.....................$6.95

ADDITIONAL COLLECTIONS

AT THE LAKE
by Elvina Pearce
Elementary/Late Elementary Level
00131642 10 Solos and Duets.....$7.99

CHRISTMAS FOR TWO
by Dan Fox
Early Intermediate Level
00290069 13 Duets....................$8.99

CHRISTMAS JAZZ
by Mike Springer
Intermediate Level
00296525 6 Solos.......................$8.99

COUNTY RAGTIME FESTIVAL
by Fred Kern
Intermediate Level
00296882 7 Solos.......................$7.99

LITTLE JAZZERS
by Jennifer Watts
Elementary/Late Elementary Level
00154573 9 Solos.......................$8.99

PLAY THE BLUES!
by Luann Carman
Early Intermediate Level
00296357 10 Solos.....................$9.99

ROLLER COASTERS & RIDES
by Jennifer & Mike Watts
Intermediate Level
00131144 8 Duets.......................$8.99

HAL•LEONARD®
www.halleonard.com

Prices, contents, and availability subject to change without notice.